THE BILLINGSLY FAMILY HISTORY

England to America

By

Katherine Fletcher

BILLINGSLEY FAMILY HISTORY

The Billingsley Family came from Shropshire England to America. This
book covers Nineteen Generations.   They lived in Maryland, Virginia,
North Carolina, Tennessee, Mississippi and Texas.   The American line
started in Maryland. This family went through many hardships and life
events yet not only survived but thrived in this new country called
America.

GENERATION ONE:

Voyle Billingsly born 1910 in Texas and and Helen Purvis was born in Priddy, TX

lived in Stephenville, TX when Leslie was born.
His birthplace was Dublin, TX / He was a mechanic.

GENERATION TWO

Walter Kimbro Billingsly (1875-1958) Born on October 16, 1875 in St. Augustine, TX and died June 10, 1958 in Dublin, TX.

He married first to Cuma Pernece Halford in 1896 in Waco, McLennan, TX

They had children: Pearl (1900) and Lucius (1903-1908)

* In 1900 he lived in Justice Precinct 3, Mills, TX
He married second to Gussie Lee Johnson in 1908

Gussie Lee Johnson

(1886-1980) was born December 22, 1886 in Alabama. She died
Octover 17, 1980 in Erath County, TX.

Their children were:

Voyle (1910-)
Oleta (1911 -)

GENERATION THREE

Edward Council Billingsly (1848-1918)

and Delilah Elizabeth Landrum (1851-1918)

Edward

 Birth 15 Jun 1848 in Pontotoc, Pontotoc, Mississippi, United States
 Death 18 May 1918 in Blanco, Blanco, Texas, United States
According to his death certificate below he died of Chronic
Bronchitis. He was a farmer.

DELILA ELIZABETH LANDRUM BILLINGSLY

Birth: Apr., 1851
Mississippi, USA
Death: Aug. 22, 1918

Blanco
Blanco County
Texas, USA

The Daughter of Azariah Kimbro Landrum and Marth Ann Tudor.

Upon the death Upon the death of his son and daughter-in-law, Edward and Delila moved to Blanco from Fredericksberg, Texas to raise their grandchildren. His son that died is Walter Marshall and here's his family pictures. Apparently his son and wife died in 1908 of a tragedy, murder / suicide. These are the children that Edward and and Delila raised.

HERE'S THE STORY OF HOW WILLIAM MARSHALL AND WIFE DIED

AS TOLD BY A WITNESS, THEIR DAUGHTER ALTA MAE

"In the spring of 1992, Alta Mae Billingsley (Byers), her nephew Bruce & Artell Billingsley and myself went on a road trip to Blanco, Johnson City and Hye, Texas.

Aunt Alta is forever remembered by me as always having a big smile, giving a loving hug and being interested in everything about whoever she was with. She was never tall and at 88, she was getting smaller but still as animated as ever.

So, even though I was in my thirties and had a full time business and family and all the things pulling at me that this world throws at you, I took off the day to go on a field trip.

One of the best days of my life and a time I can not describe well enough.

My father picked me up in Boerne and we then went off to Blanco by way of highway 46 east to 281 north. As we drove along, Aunt Alta talked about the past and I have to say that I have forgotten much more than I remember. I really did not know what was in store for me but getting the chance to be with her was what I was in the car for.

As we came to the south end of Blanco and 281 starts to go downhill, we took a slight right down a road and probably less than a mile later there was a cemetery on the left which lay between this road and 281 not too far off in the distance.

We went out and the history of the Billingsley family started flowing from Aunt Alta. There are a number of Billingsley grave sites in this cemetery but the one that stood out was Lucius Billingsley. Aunt Alta said that he died at the age of 22 while busting broncs near Blanco. She said that his foot got stuck in the stirrup as he was thrown from the saddle and the horse dragged and kicked him and he was torn up on barbed wire. She pointed out the graves of others and at that point, I did not understand why.

The next stop was Johnson City and where we had lunch before going to the big city of Hye. It was here that we stopped to have lunch and Aunt Alta told me the story of her parents for the very first (and only) time.

In the late summer of 1980, her father, William Billingsley, and brother Floyd Billingsley had been working the family farm outside the town of Hye and fairly close to a small existing church with a cemetery. It had been very hot and her father suffered a severe heat stroke. They somehow got word out and the doctor made the house call. After diagnosing the heat stroke, he told Josephine Billingsley that her husband could not be saved. He did not have that long to live.

Aunt Alta's eyes were tearing up as she told this story. She was about 4 years old at this time and 84 years later, could still vividly remember this story. She said that her mother and father loved each other very, very much and were very dependent upon one another. Her mother, upon hearing the news that her husband was going to die, went to him and told him that she loved him, did not know how she would be able to make it without him and how she so wished she could go with him.

Later that day or the next but in the afternoon, William got up from his bed, Aunt Alta described him as being delirious and out of his mind, and he told Josephine that she was going with him and at that he pulled out a gun and shot her in the stomach. He then went outside the house and shot himself.

Her mother fell to floor and Alta embraced her. As her mother was dying, she stroked Alta and Alta remembers how beautiful her mother was with her long flowing hair and her comb that was on the floor and she could not forget the blood, there was so much of it. Her mother faded away as her brother Floyd came running in from the fields where he was working (you have to remember tht he was just a young boy).

Her father, did not die until the next day.

After that, her grandparents came in to take care of them and moved into Blanco.

 We then went on to see the farm that is located several miles south of Hye off of 290 between Johnson City and Fredericksberg.

The remnants of the homestead could still be seen and I found a couple of pieces of an old wood stove. The graves of Momma and Pappa are located in a small cemetery next to a very small church nearby."

GENERATION FOUR

Edward Council Billingsly (1813-1885) and Winifred Manning Brookshire (1812-1885)

He married in 1831 in Blount Co, Alabama

EDWARD COUNCIL

>   Birth 04 April 1811 in , Cumberland Co, Kentucky, USA
>   Death 17 July 1885 in , Shelby Co, Texas, USA

WINIFRED MANNING BROOKSHIRE

>   Birth 11 January 1813 in , Randolph Co, North Carolina, USA
>   Death 06 February 1901 in , Shelby Co, Texas, USA

Her parents were James Brookshire (1783-1864) and Sallie O Ha Yah Graves (1790-1855)
Sallie is 100% Choctaw or Cherokee.

Their children:

John BILLINGSLEY- 1832 - 1848
Elizabeth Emaline BILLINGSLEY - 1835 - 1883
Sarah BILLINGSLEY - 1836 - 1900
Mary BILLINGSLEY - 1837 - 1888
Courtney Prudence BILLINGSLEY - 1840 - 1926
JERMINA ARMINDA BILLINGSLEY - 1842 - 1900
 William Mannering Mang BILLINGSLEY - 1844 - 1888
James Thomas BILLINGSLEY - 1845 - 1945
Edward Council BILLINGSLEY - 1848 - 1918
Martha R BILLINGSLEY - 1850-1931

California Callie BILLINGSLEY - 1852 -
Joseph BILLINGSLEY - 1853 - 1929
Winnie Isabella Tip BILLINGSLEY - 1855-1936
Nancy Jane Emma BILLINGSLEY

GENERATION FIVE:

Thomas Billingsley (1782-1849) and

Nancy Courtney Allen (1783-1843)

THOMAS

Birth 30 December 1782 in , Onslow Co, North Carolina, USA

Death 1849 in , Pontotoc Co, Mississippi, USA

Born in Onslow Nc Jacksonvlle on 1782 to Samuel Billingsley and Mary Griffith. Thomas married **Martha Blackwood** and had a child. Thomas married **Jane Hoodenpyle** and had 7 children. Thomas married **Nancy Courtney Allen** and had 13 children. He passed away on 1849 in Missorui.

He married Nancy in 1801 and lived in Marion, Perry Alabama in 1850

NANCY

Birth 1783 in , , North Carolina, USA

Death 1843 in , Morgan Co, Alabama, USA

She lived in Randals, Cobb, Georgia and Cumberland North Carolina.

Their children:

Nancy BILLINGSLEY -   1802 - 1870

James BILLINGSLEY -   1803 - 1889

Samuel BILLINGSLEY-   1803 - 1840

Thomas BILLINGSLEY =   1805 - 1880

Sarah BILLINGSLEY =   1810 -

EDWARD COUNCIL BILLINGSLEY -   1811 - 1885

Mary Eliza BILLINGSLEY -   1813 -

Barton BILLINGSLEY -   1815 -

Elizabeth BILLINGSLEY -   1816 -

Catherine BILLINGSLEY -   1818 -

Rebecca Courtney BILLINGSLEY -   1820 - 1870

William G BILLINGSLEY -   1822 - 1904

GENERATION SIX:

Samuel Billingsley (1747-1816)

and Mary Griffith (1753-1838)

SAMUEL

     Birth June 1747 in St Mary's County, Maryland, United States
     Death April 1816 in , Bledsoe County, Tennessee, United States
Married 1772 to Mary Griffith in Guilford, North Carolina
Served in the American Revolution.

MARY

     Birth 01 September 1753 in , , North Carolina, USA

     Death 01 September 1838 in , Bledsoe Co, Tennessee, USA

Samuel Billingsly was born in St. Mary's County, Maryland in 1747.
He moved to Baltimore with his parents in 1758 and then to Guilford
County, NC in 1768. He married Mary Griffith. Samuel got a portion of
his father's estate when he married.   He got 300 acres of land in
Onslow County, NC. He also served in the American Revolution in 1781
with Captain J. Sharpe's Co. He received land of 100 acres in
Sullivan County, Tennessee.   He later moved to Sequachie Valley in
Bledso County, TN. He was a Mason and a Baptist. He died in 1816 at
home.

Their children:

James BILLINGSLEY -   1772 - 1772

Sarah Sally BILLINGSLEY -   1773 - 1854

Mary BILLINGSLEY -   1773 -

Samuel BILLINGSLEY -   1775 - 1857

Mary BILLINGSLEY -   1777 -

William BILLINGSLEY -   1779 - 1819

Jeptha BILLINGSLEY -   1780 - 1863

John BILLINGSLEY -   1781 - 1856

THOMAS BILLINGSLEY -   1782 - 1849

Amanda BILLINGSLEY -   1784 -

Elijah BILLINGSLEY -   1786 - 1893

Elizabeth BILLINGSLEY -   1786 -

Elyath BILLINGSLEY -   1786 - 1853

Sarah BILLINGSLEY -   1788 -

Nancy BILLINGSLEY -   1790 -

Rebecca BILLINGSLEY -   1804 -

GENERATION SEVEN:

James Billingsley (1726-1776)

and Elizabeth Crabtree (1720-1832)

James

Birth April 1726 in St Mary's County, Maryland, United States

Death Apr 1776 in Hung as a Revolutionist by the Torres, Guilford, North Carolina, United States

He married in 1748.

Elizabeth

Birth 13 December 1720 in St Johns Parish, Baltimore County, Maryland, United States

Death 1832 at _**age 113**_ in McMinn County, Tennessee, United States

She was married in St. John's Parish Baltimore County, Maryland

Her parents were William Crabtree (1682-1756) and Jane Halstead (1687-1759).

Her father was the first immigrant of this the CRABTREE line.
William   Birth 06 March 1682 in Broughton, County Yorkshire, ,
England, United Kingdom and   Death 10 September 1756 in Kingsville,
Baltimore County, Maryland, United States .

Here is a story about JAMES and his tragic death

"he James Billingsley Chapter, NSDAR, was organized March 19, 1963
with twelve charter members. Frances Tidmore is the last original
charter member still active in the chapter. The Chapter is named for
JAMES BILLINGSLEY, a patriot who lost his life when loyalists to the
British cause invaded his home in April 1776. He had been continually
harassed by these Tories, when they invaded his home and asked for
money. On being told he had none, they took him to a near by tree and
hung him. (This statement came from his wife, Elizabeth Crabtree, who
made notes of his death in the family bible. As she lived to know many
of her great-grand children, she often spoke and repeated the tragic
death of her husband to them.) Born in St. Mary's County, Maryland, in
1726, he was the son of William and Mary Sumner Billingsley. He
married Elizabeth Crabtree in 1747. They moved to Guilford County,
North Carolina, about 1768. His sons Samuel, James, and John served as
soldiers in the American Revolution. One of his descendants, Captain
Jesse Billingsley, fought with General Sam Houston at the Battle of
San Jacinto and is credited by the historian, Frank Dobie, with having
given Texas her battle cry: "Remember the Alamo!"

Here's another story from ancestry.com

    JAMES   BILLINGSLEY -

    Born St. Marys County, Maryland. in 1726. He was legatee in his
father's will in 1745. He married prior to 1747 Elizabeth Crabtree,
born 1726 in Maryland. They moved to Baltimore County, Maryland about
1758 where they resided to about 1768 then moved to Guilford County,
North Carolina. He appears to have owned considerable land but there
does not appear any deeds to account for it. In 1771 he appears as a
signer to a petition asking clemency for John Pugh and Thomas Welborn
who appear to have been associated with the Insurrectionists. (N. C.
Rec. Vol. ix, 26, 26, 29, 30.)

    When the Revolution began he became quite active in aiding the
American cause, sent his sons into the service and incurred the enmity

of the Tories of the vicinity in particular. He was continually harassed by them until the year 1776 when they invaded his home and asked for money, on being told he had none they took him to a near by tree and hung him. This statement comes from his wife who made note of his death in the family bible, and as she lived to know many of her great grand children she often repeated the tragic death of her husband to them.

One of these, the son of John Billingsley, Junior, heard the story, and it was also often repeated to him by his grand father and as he was a lad of some 15 years of age at the time of the death of his grand father he wrote all of it down at the time. Before his death he wrote out all that he had made note of into a complete record of the family for his children.

James Billingsley was killed in April 1776.

This is an actual sketch of the hanging

JAMES WILL:

He dated his will 25 Jan. 1776 and it was probated at the May Term of court 1776, an abstract follows:

Item: In consideration of my children that is in being already portioned, that is to say, James, Elizabeth, Claranna, Samuel, and John, to each 2 shillings and 6 pence.

Item: To son, William H., one bed & furniture to be recorded in with his equal part with the following children, to wit: Martha & Walter & Bazil.

Item: To Martha; my daughter, one bed & furniture, one chist & one Cow to be in part her equal share in the list above mentioned.

Item: My two youngest sons, Walter & Bazel, plantation when they come of age, & that they share an equal part of the movable estate with others of my so last mentioned fore children.

Item: To my well beloved wife during her widowhood one bed & furniture, one horse, one mare, two cows & calves & Plantation, and if a widow when my sons come of age for her to have her right in the land so long as a widow, this exclusive of her one third in movable estate, said wife to be executrix.

Item: To daughter Claranna, value of 3 pounds of estate exclusive of the above 2 shillings 6 pence.

This will witnessed by Teldeau Lane and William Hamer.

Elizabeth survived him many years, moved to Tennessee with her sons and resided many years with her son, John, in Warren County, Kentucky. About 1838 she made the trip to McMinn County, Tennessee to spend a while with her son, Walter, she did not long survive this trip and died early in 1839 aged 113 years. Walter was given the family Bible a part of the record he filed with his claim for a pension.

"The Billingsley Family in America"Author: Harry Alexander DavisPublication: 1936

Children of James Billingsley and Elizabeth Crabtree

Samuel Billingsley (1747-1816,TN) m. Mary Griffith (1753-1838)

James Billingsley (1749-?)

Elizabeth Billingsley (1751-?) m. Teldeau Lane

John Billingsley (1754, St. Mary's County, MD-1844, KY) m. Jean Milsap (?-1842, KY)

Claranna Billingsley (1756-?) m. William Hamer

William Henry Billingsley (1758-?)

Martha Billingsley (1760-1786) was second wife to William Hamer

Walter Billingsley (1761-1850)

Bazil Billingsley (1764-1831)

GENERATION EIGHT:

William W. Billingsley (1691-1745) and Mary Sumner (1691-1740)

William

     Birth Nov 1691 in Calvert, Cecil, Maryland, United States,

    Death 11 Aug 1745 in St Marys, St Mary's, Maryland, United States

Mary

     Birth 1691 in Calvert, Maryland, United States

    Death Dec 1740 in St Mary, Maryland, United States

THEIR HOUSE:

Their children:

Siare Billingsley	-1745
Mary Sumner Billingsley	1718-1759
William Sumner Billingsley	1720-1758
Ann Billingsley	1723 -
John Billingsley	1723-1740
Ann Billingsley	1724-
JAMES BILLINGSLEY	**1726-1776**
Margaret Billingsley	1728-1740
Elizabeth Billingsley	1729-
Francis Billingsley	1735-1799
Sias Billingsley	1738-1817

GENERATION NINE:

William Billingsley (1670-1713) and Clearanna Bowles (1671-1716)

WILLIAM

Born Calvert County, Maryland October 1670

Married 1rst to Sarah Ann (1652-1712) Richmond, Essex, Virginia, They had child Samuel 1768-1815

   Death 1712 in Richmond, Wise, Virginia, United States

Married Clearanna in 1691 in Cecil, Maryland

CLEARANNA

   Birth 1671 in Calvert, Maryland, United States

   Death Jul 1716 in Calvert, Cecil, Maryland, United States

STORY OF WILLIAM

WILLIAM BILLINGSLEY

Born Calvert County, Maryland October 1670. He moved to Virginia with his parents and then returned to Calvert County with them in 1675. He married prior to 1691 Clearanna Bowler, born Maryland 167-. She is believed to be a daughter of Valentine Bowler.

He was given 100 acres of land called "Addition," at the time of his marriage by his father and he disposed of the same before 1700 as Rent Rolls show it was possessed at that date by Benjamin Ball. In 1700 he is listed on a Rent Roll as possessing 100 acres of land part of a 350 acre tract surveyed for George Young in February 1680 at head of Bottle Creek. On 5 July 1704136 acres of land were surveyed for William Billingsley and called "Billingsley's Swamp" on the North side. of Bottle Creek and adjoining land of John Wood. (Lib. D5, fol.170.) He acquired other holdings of land tho no deeds have been found concerning the same. In the will of Richard Johns of Calvert County probated 14 June 1717/18: item: to my grand son Richard, son of my deceased son Abraham, two tracts made over to the testator by William Billingsley, i.e., 136 acres called "Billingsley's Swamp," and 150 acres called "Friendship Rectified."

In 1700 William Creed and William Billingsley appraised the estate of John Carmody. (Test. Proc. xviiiB-47.) On 17 Sept. 1706 William Billingsley and William Williams, appraised and inventoried the estate of Andrew Graham. (Test Proc. xixC-81.)

He died intestate latter part of July 1716 and his estate administered 4 Aug. 1716 by Clearanna, his widow, with James Cobb and William Billingsley, Jr. as bondsmen for 100 pounds. On 10 Jan. 1716/17 is an - account and July 1717 is final account rendered by William Billingsley, Jr. Date of the death of Clearanna is not known tho the final return of administration returned by her son indicates she was deceased.

Their children;

William W. Billingsley (1691,Calvert Co. MD - bef. 1745, St.
    Mary's Co, MD) m. Mary Sumner (1695-?)
Clearanna Billingsley (1693-aft. 1734) m. Gilly
Bowles Billingsley (1694-bef. 1745) m. Rachel (?-aft. 1745)
Samuel Billingsley (1696-?) m. 2) Mary Wilmouth (widow)
Ann Elizabeth Billingsley (1699?)

THe WILL OF WILLIAM:

Will of William Billingsley, 1745, St. Mary's County, MD In the name of God, Amen. I William Billingsley of St. Mary's County, in the Province of Maryland, being of Perfect Memory thanks be to God for the same tho sick and weak in Body and not knowing how soon a Change may come, knowing we are all mortal, I make this my Last Will and Testament revoking all others heretofore made in any kind whatsoever as followeth.

First, I give my Soul into the hands of Almighty God that gave it to me and my Body I recommnd to the Earth to be Buried at the Discretion of my Executor hereafter named.

First I desire that Funeral Charges Just debts to be Paid then the rest of my estate as followeth.

Item: I give and bequeath unto my daughter Mary Wood an hogg about two years old.

Item: I give and bequeath unto my daughter Ann Hardesty one Ewe and Lamb.

Item: I give and bequeath unto my son William Billingsley and my son James Billingsley my two negroes Sambo and Ben. I also desire that my son William make his choice of them by Christmas after my death. I also desire that my son James have a young horse named Spark that I promised him for learning his younger brothers and sisters to read and that he comply with this part of the agreement.

Item: I give and bequeath unto my five younger children, Margaret, Clare, Francis, Siare and Elizabeth all the rest of my personal estate to be equally divided amongst them or the survivors such as shall come to age to recieve the same and

lastly I hereby ordain and appoint my son Willim Billingsley Executor of this my Last Will and Testament. In Witness whereof I have hereunto set my hand and seal this 11th day of Aug. Anno Dom. 1745.

Witnesses:Rachel BillingsleyJames Kuch

GENERATION TEN

John Billingsley and Sarah Ann Francis Billingsley

John Billingsley (-1686) m. Mary (1669-1709/1710)

Their children:

John 1647-1693
Sara 1652-1712
William Billingsley (1670-1716) m. Clearanna Bowles (ca. 1667-1717)

Sarah Agatha Billingsley (1672/73-?)
Elizabeth Billingsley (1675-1752)
Susannah Billingsley (1678/1679-?)
Walter Billingsley (1685-aft. 1734)

GENERATION ELEVEN:

John Billingsley (1647-1693) and Sarah Ann (I think her name is Brown) showing father William Brown in Richmond, VA. (1652, VA-?)

Birth: 1647

Death: 1693

John Billingsley was the son of Francis and Ann Billingsley. He was born in Rotterdam, Holland in 1647 and he died at sea during a storm.

The book '17th Century Colonial Ancestors", Volume 1, page 25 shows John Billingsley (1647-1693) as a maritime trader and land owner.

Burial: Body lost at sea during storm

SARAH ANN BROWN

She was born 1652 in Virginia and died at 61 years.

Her father was William Brown of Richmond VA.

GENERATION TWELVE

Francis Billingsley (1620, County Salop, England - died 1684 Calvert Co, MD) m. Ann ? born around 1620 Holland / died 1688 Calvert County, MD.

Francis Billingsley came to the United States with his brothers John and James.

Brought wife and son, John to Maryland, from Virginia

BILLINGSLEY of MARYLAND

Francis Billingsley, a Member of the Lower House from Calvert County, Maryland, was born ca 1620, at Shropshire, Salop County, England; died 1684, Selby Clifts, Calvert Co., Maryland; married 1646-1647, in Rotterdam, Holland, Ann (proven by Prov. Court Liber FF Folio 652 - Hall of Records, Annapolis, Md.), born 1620-25 in Holland; died ca 1668-70 at Selby Clifts, Calvert Co., Md. Francis Billingsley was a Planter and a Quaker. He was educated in England and resided in England, Holland and America.

Francis Billingsley received a land grant of 200 acres called "Selby Clifts" lying in the Province of Maryland by Lord Baltimore on the 26th day of November, 1650, for the transportation of Thomas Forby in 1649 from Caecilius into Maryland. Dec. 5, 1654, Francis Billingsley was made Constable of Clifts, and ordered to be present at the next Court to take office as Constable. The last reference in Maryland Court Records to Burgess Francis Billingsley is November 1683 so we can place his death between this date and the Court held in 1684. He being a Quaker died intestate for the reason he refused to swear. (See Beese's Sufferings of the Quakers, Volume II, page 380 - Under Heading of Maryland 1658 -- "Distress On Francis Billingsley".)

Thelma Downing Pulley (Mrs. Thomas Nicholson Pulley), Oak Grove, La., had, on June 11, 1957, the following Crest and Coat of Arms Registered by the New England Historic Genealogical Society's Committee on Heraldy:

Billingsley - London and Salop

Crest: (On a mount vert) a leopard, couchant, or spotted sable

Arms: Argent, a cross sable voided of the field five estoiles in cross between four lions rampant all of the second

Children:

I.   John Billingsley, b. 1647; m. Sarah Ann Billingsley (See later).
II. Ann Billingsley, b. 1650; died young.
III. Agatha Billingsley, b. 1656; m. Thomas Paget.
IV. Francis Billingsley, Jr., b. 1653; d. 1695; m. Susanna.
V.   Edward Billingsley, b. 1658; m. Ann.
VI. Ann Eliz. Billingsley, b. 1660; m. Thomas Sadler.

John Billingsley was born 1647, in Rotterdam, Holland; died ca 1690, (lost at sea). Married Jan. 1669, in Richmond Co., Va., Sarah Ann Billingsley (1st cousin), born 1652, in Essex County, Va.; died 1712, probably in St. Mary's County, Md., daughter of William Billingsley, who was born in Salop Co., England, and his wife, Sarah Bowman, of Essex Co., Virginia, who married

Bevin, Arthur (1652-1697) Conn.; m. Mary ---. Land-
     owner.
Bevin, Richard (c1620-) Va.; m. ---. Landowner.
Bibb, Benjamin (1640-1702) Va.; m. Mary ---. Pro-
     prietor.
Biddle, William (1650-1712) N.J.; m. Sarah ( ) Kempe.
     Justice; Proprietor.
Bidlack, Christopher (1661-1740) Mass.; m. Sarah
     Fuller. Landowner.
Bidwell, John (c1620-87) Conn.; m. Sarah Wilcox.
     Landowner; Freeman.
Bigelow, John (1617-1703) Mass.; m. Mary Warren;
     Sarah Bemis.   Selectman; Military service.
Bigelow, Joshua (1655-1745) Mass.; m. Elizabeth
     Flagg. Landowner; Military service.
Bigger, James (1684-1770) Va.; m. ---. Landowner.
Biglo   SEE   Bigelow
Bilbo, Jean Jacques (-c1739) Va.; m. ---. Founder.
Biles, William (1650-1710) Pa.; m. Jane Atkinson.
     Councillor; Pennsylvania Great Charter.
Biles, William (1672-1747) Pa.; m. Sarah Langhorne.
     Proprietor; Assemblyman.
Bill, Phillip (1665-1729) Mass.; m. Mercy Houghlow.
     Military service.
Billingsley, Francis (1620-84) Md.; m. Ann ---.
     Assemblyman.
Billingsley, John (1647-93) Md.-Va.; m. Sarah ---.
     Maritime trader; Landowner.
Billingsley, William (1628-57) Va.; m. Sarah Bowman.
     Maritime trader; Landowner.
Billingsley, William (1670-1716) Md.; m. Clearanna
     Bowles. Landowner; Tax assessor.
Billington, Luke (-) Va.; m. Elisia Russell.
     Landowner.
Bingham, James (c1668-1714) Pa.; m. Ann ---. Vestry-
     man; Landowner.
Bingham, Thomas (1642-1710) Conn.; m. Mary Rudd.
     Founder.
Binns, Henry (c1622-69) Va.; m. Martha ---; Elizabeth
     Alston. Justice; Commissioner.

SEXUAL ASSAULT STORY OF HIS WIFE ANN

Maryland Archives - online unknown file number, MD Archives, Volume 57, preface 30:

Two men charged with rape, although this word is not actually used any-where in this record, came before the court. In both instances the accused were acquitted. William Key of Selby's Cliff, Calvert County, was charged with assault by force and arms and of ravishing against her will Ann, the wife of Frances Billingsley of the same place. The assault was said to have taken place in her husband's chamber, and the indictment declared that it was an offence contrary to the statute passed in the 13th year of the reign of Edward I. It is of interest to know that the statute of Westminster II, 13 Edward I (1285), made rape a felony with the benefit of clergy, while the statute passed in 1575 in the reign of Elizabeth, which one would suppose had supplanted the earlier act, took away the benefit of clergy. Key, who could probably read, was pre-sented under the earlier and milder statute. The trial was conducted in a pecu-liar way, in that Key, indicted for rape, and a certain Thomas Corker, indicted for murder, had their cases, according to the record, heard consecutively by the same jury, which then retired and brought in at the same time verdicts in both cases. Key leaded not guilty and asked a jury trial. The jury of "life and death" of which Joseph Horsley was foreman, after hearing the evidence of the al-leged victim and of another woman and two men, brought in a verdict of not guilty, and the jury "being askt if he did not fly for it answered not to our knowledge"—a question asked to show whether the accused had attempted escape, because, whether found guilty or not, attempted flight by an accused person carried with it forfeiture of goods and chattels. The accused does not seem to have been called to testify in his own behalf. Key was then cleared by a proclamation. As the record does not disclose the evidence we are left to suspect that perhaps the jury may have felt, that whatever had occurred was perhaps not entirely "against the will" of Mrs. Billingsley (pp. 353, 354, 356, 357).

Their Children:

John BILLINGSLEY,   b. 1647,   d. 1693 (Age 46 years)

Ann BILLINGSLEY,   b. 1650, VA at this location,   d. Yes, date unknown

Francis BILLINGSLEY,   b. 1653, Calvert Co., MD Find all individuals with events at this location,   d. 10 Jun 1695, Calvert Co., MD (Age 42 years)

Agtha BILLINGSLEY,   b. Abt 1656, MD

Edward BILLINGSLEY,   b. 1658, Calvert Co., MD   d. 1708   (Age 50 years)

Ann Elizabeth BILLINGSLEY,   b. Abt 1660, VA

GENERATION THIRTEEN

John Billingsley (1587-before 1659) and Agatha ? (1593-1666

JOHN

Born in Shropshire England and died in Holland. His wife Agatha also died in Holland.

Their children;

John BILLINGSLEY,   b. 1612
Agatha BILLINGSLEY,   b. 1614
James BILLINGSLEY,   b. 1616
Thomas BILLINGSLEY,   b. Abt 1618, Shropshire Co., ENGLAND Find all individuals with events at this location
Francis BILLINGSLEY,   b. 1620, Astley, Shropshire, ENGLAND Find all individuals with events at this location,   d. 1684, Calvert Co., MD Find all individuals with events at this location (Age 64 years)
Bridgett BILLINGSLEY,   b. Abt 1622
Frances BILLINGSLEY,   b. 1624
Joanne BILLINGSLEY,   b. 1626
William BILLINGSLEY,   b. 1628, Shropshire Co., ENGLAND d. Dec 1657 (Age 29 years)
Mary BILLINGSLEY,   b. Abt 1630,   d. HOLLAND
Walter BILLINGSLEY,   b. Abt 1632

GENERATION FOURTEEN

Francis Billingsley and Bridgett Vernon
John Billingsley (ca. 1549, Astley Shropshire, Englan and died bef. 1659, Holland)

Bridgett Vernon's father was Sir Thomas Vernon from Haslingden, Com. Chester, ENGLAND Check out the long lineage of the Vernons from 1052 http://www.tudorplace.com.ar/VERNON.htm

Their children

```
Dorothy BILLINGSLEY,    b. 1575
Francis BILLINGSLEY,    b. Abt 1578
Marye BILLINGSLEY,    b. Abt 1580
Frances BILLINGSLEY,    b. Abt 1582
Janne BILLINGSLEY,    b. Abt 1584
Thomas BILLINGSLEY,    b. Abt 1586
John BILLINGSLEY,    b. Abt 1587, Shropshire Co., ENGLAND   d. Bef
1659, HOLLAND
Margaret BILLINGSLEY,    b. Abt 1589
Jane BILLINGSLEY,    b. Abt 1591
William BILLINGSLEY,    b. Abt 1593
Rachel BILLINGSLEY,    b. Abt 1595
Judeth BILLINGSLEY,    b. Abt 1595
Benjamin BILLINGSLEY,    b. Abt 1600
Edward BILLINGSLEY,    b. Abt 1602
Bridgett BILLINGSLEY,    b. Abt 1604
```

GENERATION FIFTEEN

John Billingsley the Edler and Frances Acton

John was born 1525 in Astley Shropshire, England.

Francis 1549, England-aft. 1623, England

 Frances Acton was born circa 1527 at Aldenham, Shropshire, England.
She married John Billingsley the Elder, son of William Billingsley Jr.
and Ciceleye (?), on 26 February 1544 at Astley Abbots, Shropshire,
England. As of 26 February 1544,her married name was Frances
Billingsley (Acton).

Their Children:

Janne BILLINGSLEY

Ciceleye BILLINGSLEY

Francis BILLINGSLEY,   b. Abt 1549, ENGLAND Find all individuals with
events at this location

GENERATION SIXTEEN

William Billingsley and Ciceleye ?

William Billingsley Jr. was born circa 1495 at Salop, England. He married Ciceleye (?) circa 1523.

Family

   Ciceleye (?) b. c 1495

Their Children

   John Billingsley the Elder+ b. 1525

   William Billingsley b. c 1527

   Richard Billingsley b. c 1529

   Joanne Billingsley b. c 1531

GENERATION SEVENTEEN

Roger Billingsley / born maybe around 1525

Canturbury, Com. Kent, ENGLAND

Children: William and Roger

GENERATION EIGHTEEN:

Roger Billingsley of Com. Salop, ENG / born maybe around 1500

Had child: Roger

GENERATION NINETEEN

Roger Billingsley born 1481 in Com. Salop, England / lived in Shropshire, England

His child: Roger

CHECK OUT THESE WEBSITES FOR MORE INFORMATION

http://www.thebillingsleys.net/theBillingsleys/THE%20BILLINGSLEY%20FAM
ILY.htm

A WIKIPEDIA PAGE ABOUT BILLINGSLEY, SHROPSHIRE ENGLAND

http://en.wikipedia.org/wiki/Billingsley,_Shropshire

They could have taken their original name from the village name. Very
common to do that.

FAMILY NOTES